ADVENT
PARISH
PROGRAMME

ADVENT
PARISH
PROGRAMME

Participant's Handbook

SEAMUS HEANEY

Veritas Publications

First published 1987 by
Veritas Publications
7-8 Lower Abbey Street
Dublin 1

NIHIL OBSTAT
Richard Sherry, D.D.
Censor Deputatus

IMPRIMATUR
✠ Joseph A. Carroll
Dublin Diocesan Administrator

Acknowledgements
Quotations from *The New Jerusalem Bible,* published and copyright 1985 by Darton,
Longman & Todd Ltd. and Doubleday & Co. Inc.: excerpts from the English
translation of *The Roman Missal* © 1973, International Committee on English in
the Liturgy, Inc. (ICEL); excerpts from *Vatican Council II: Conciliar and Post
Conciliar Documents,* edited by Austin Flannery, O.P.; excerpt from the English
translation of *A Book of Prayers* © 1982, ICEL; English translations of the
Apostles' Creed and Gloria Patri by the International Consultation on English
texts.

Cover design by Jim Kilgarriff

ISBN: 0 86217 269 1

Typesetting by Printset & Design Ltd.
Printed in Ireland.

CONTENTS

INTRODUCTION

Welcome to the Advent Parish Programme. At Christmas we celebrate the birth of Jesus. Jesus' birth in Bethlehem was a wonderful expression of God's love for all people and a new beginning for the human race. Each time Christmas is celebrated, God offers his love and mercy to every man and woman. He wants to enter into the life of every individual and to reveal his love for them in a new way. Do you have a desire to know God's love? Do you wish to respond to the invitation given to everybody at the end of the New Testament? - 'Then let all who are thirsty come; all who want it may have the water of life, and have it free' *(Revelations 22:17)*.

Perhaps you are thinking, 'But I am such an unworthy person'. We must never allow ourselves to think that we are too unimportant, too small or too sinful for God to speak to us and us to him. Our very lack of expectancy can rob us of God's blessing. It is almost like saying, 'I know that it is possible but I've never heard him speak to me so I suppose that's how it's meant to be'. By thinking in this way we can lose any hope or expectancy that God will show his love for us in a personal way. This can create a real obstacle. Unless we are ready both to believe that God loves us as a Father and to act on that belief, we can hinder the development of a personal relationship with him.

The Advent programme is an opportunity for you 'to come and take the water'. God's desire is to show the depth of his love for you. He wants both to speak and listen to you and work in your life. However, this will not happen without your active involvement. Jesus offers the drink - his life and truth - but it is up to you to receive it and take it into your system, believe it and act on it.

This handbook is a guide for you as you go through the programme. Before you begin, turn to God and ask him for the gift of faith. Ask him to give you a sense of expectancy and promise him that you will believe in his love for you. If you open your mind and heart to him you can expect that God will work in your life this Advent.

Over the four weeks of the programme there will be a weekly meeting at which a talk will be given and opportunity for discussion provided. However, your active involvement will not end there. In this handbook you will find a short Scripture passage for each day of the programme. You are recommended to read and meditate on this passage during your prayer time. After each passage there is a short meditation to help you. In addition you are given 'A Structure for Prayer' (pp. 9-10). This is a practical guide to help you establish a practice of daily personal prayer. This is different from the practice of saying a few set prayers or even praying as you go around the house or on your way to work. It involves going to a quiet place for at least ten minutes and using the elements suggested in 'A Structure for Prayer'.

When you first attempt to pray in this way you may discover that it is not easy. You may become distracted and allow your mind to wander. With so many demands on your time you may even be tempted to skip prayer altogether. To do this would be to miss the blessings God wants to give you. If you are faithful to daily prayer you can be sure you will receive the blessings God has promised. As prayer becomes an integral part of your life you will begin to experience the presence of God and enter into a real dialogue with him. And you will soon notice the effects it will have on your life.

There are also other ways through which you can deepen your awareness of the season of Advent. Some ideas are included in a special section of your booklet entitled 'Family Activities for Advent'. (See pp. 44-49.) Some of these activities can be done by your family (or the people you live with) and some can be done by individuals. It is important that you read this section carefully and decide which activities are most suitable for your situation. You may wish to discuss with your family which activities would appeal to them.

A STRUCTURE FOR PRAYER

1. Choose a TIME
Make it a definite time dedicated only to prayer. Try to make it the best time you can find.

2. Choose a PLACE
It should be free from distractions.

3. Go over the BASIC FACTS in your mind
— Sign of the Cross.
— Examination of Conscience.
  Forgive and be forgiven. (Matthew 5:23; 6:14-15)
— Pray the Creed or pray over in your mind the basic truths of revelation.
  * God created you out of love and loves you always.
    (Genesis 1:7-31; 1 John 4:10-11)
  * God sent Jesus who gives us life.
    (John 3:16; Ephesians 2:4-5)
  * Jesus died and rose, conquering sin and death.
    (Romans 5:12-18; 1 Corinthians 15:20-26)
  * Jesus promised to be with us and so gave us the Holy Spirit.
    (John 14:16,26; 16:7; Acts 2:1-11)
  * Jesus intercedes for us constantly in heaven.
    (Romans 8:34; Hebrews 7:25; 1 John 2:1)
  * Jesus is coming again.
    (Matthew 16:27;25:34)
— Assent to these truths. Consciously say "yes" to them daily.

4. PRAISE GOD
He is worthy of all praise. (Psalm 22;95;136)

5. Ask God QUESTIONS
— Read the Scripture passage and meditation for the day.
— Read them again slowly, underlining the passages that strike you.
— Ask God questions: 'What does this mean for my life, Lord?' *(Matthew 7:7)*.
— Recall them during the day. *(Colossians 3:16)*

6. LISTEN for an answer
Expect to hear from God:
— within yourself;
— from Scripture;
— during the day.

7. RESPOND to God
Do this by:
— asking for forgiveness;
— praying for wisdom;
— praying for others.

(The Scripture passages suggested in 'A Structure for Prayer' may be found in your Bible. They are also given on pages 50-52 of this handbook.)

POINTS TO REMEMBER

* Begin your prayer time by going over 'A Structure for Prayer'.

* Read the Scripture passages and meditations for each day which are given in this handbook.

* Use a good readable translation of the Bible. If you don't have a suitable edition why not buy one now? Members of the team will be able to help you with your choice.

* If you are using *The Word Among Us,* read the Scripture passage and daily meditation.

* Ask the Lord for a thought that can direct, inspire and give new life to your day.

* Use a notebook to write down thoughts that strike you as you read Scripture and ask God questions that occur to you.

These suggestions should help you in your daily prayer, but most important is the desire to praise, adore and worship God and to learn from him.

OUTLINE OF PRESENTATION 1:
SONS AND DAUGHTERS OF GOD

On the first Sunday of Advent the Gospel warns us to 'watch' and 'stay awake'. What are the dangers about which we are being warned? They are dangers that concern gaining or losing eternal salvation.

THE WORK OF CREATION

God created the world and everything in it. Human beings were the crown of God's creation, made in his own image and likeness. (See Genesis 1:26-27.) He intended them for a special destiny. They were to be his sons and daughters and were to share his happiness for all eternity. (See Ephesians 1:4-5.) God's desire was that all men and women should live in intimate relationship with him. However, this privileged position was lost through sin. God, in his love, made it possible for this relationship to be restored by sending his Son into the world. (See John 1:1-3.) His birth was a new beginning for the human race.

OUR DIGNITY AS CHILDREN OF GOD

Jesus died and rose from the dead, thus restoring our lost dignity. As children of God we have rights and privileges, including the right to come into God's presence. (See Ephesians 3:12.) When we are aware of our rights and privileges we can live our lives in accordance with our true dignity and have a sense of peace and security. If we look for our security in what other people think of us we will be disappointed. But even if we forget that God is our Father he never forgets that we are his children. (See Luke 18:11-32.) When we turn away from him he awaits our return and wants to clothe us with the dignity we have lost.

KNOWING OUR TRUE IDENTITY

It is only through Jesus that we can come to know God as our Father. (See Colossians 1:15; Matthew 11:27; Hebrews 10:19-23.) God's desire is that we live in intimate relationship with him. (See Isaiah 55:1.) Prayer and Scripture are the gifts God has given us to enable us to come to know him. Jesus said: 'Stay awake, praying at all times....' *(Luke 21:36)*. Jesus desires that prayer be an important part of our lives.

DECISIONS ABOUT PRAYER AND SCRIPTURE

Prayer should be so necessary for our lives that we will not let a day pass in which we do not pray. We need to choose a time which we will dedicate solely to prayer. We need to choose a place which will be free from interruption.

It is easy to settle for a knowledge of Jesus that is little more than historical. Through prayer and Scripture our knowledge begins to come alive. This handbook is a practical guide to enable you to pray and read Scripture every day.

---

* During the coming week read over this outline each day.
* Look up the Scripture passages listed.
* Ask the Holy Spirit to help you to understand what you read.

SCRIPTURE READINGS AND MEDITATIONS - WEEK I

DAY 1

(Isaiah 44:1-3)
And now listen, Jacob my servant, Israel whom I have chosen. Thus says the Lord who made you, who formed you in the womb; he will help you. Do not be afraid, Jacob my servant, Jeshurun whom I have chosen. For I shall pour out water on the thirsty soil and streams on the dry ground.

Very often our lives can seem like they are going around in endless circles, like a merry-go-round always on the move but never really getting anywhere. Why not stop on this, the first day of the Advent programme, and ask the Holy Spirit to enlighten your mind about the Scripture reading from Isaiah? This Word was not just spoken to Jacob. Before you were created it was God's plan that you should hear these words personally addressed to you. God is asking you 'to listen'. You can expect to hear him speak to your heart. He wants you to know that you are not a chance happening. He loves you; he has created you; he has chosen you. You owe your very existence to him. He wants you to know the truth about the way he relates to his children. As you accept this truth you will see his promises fulfilled in your life.

We suggest you make these spiritual resolutions to help you become more open to the truth God wants to teach:
1. Set aside time for personal prayer every day.
2. Read the Scripture passages and meditations given in this handbook, asking the Holy Spirit to enlighten your mind about what you read.
3. Examine your conscience and repent of the sins you find, knowing that God forgives you.

DAY 2

(Matthew 24:42-44)
So stay awake, because you do not know the day when your master is coming. You may be quite sure of this, that if the householder had known at what time of the night the burglar would come, he would have stayed awake and would not have allowed anyone to break through the wall of his house. Therefore, you too must stand ready because the Son of man is coming at an hour you do not expect.

As we get caught up in the daily routine of everyday events, it is easy to forget that our lives in this world will not go on forever. A day will inevitably arrive which will be our last. On that day Jesus will come and ask us to render an account of ourselves. Yet, in another sense, Jesus comes to us every day. He comes as the merciful judge to show us the error of our ways and as the merciful saviour who frees us from our sins and freely forgives us. When we commit ourselves to daily personal prayer and reading of Scripture we will experience Jesus coming into our lives.

When Jesus teaches his disciples about 'staying awake' he is alerting them to the need for prayerful attention to his word and his teaching. We may think that our lives, our plans and our time are our own. This is not so. We belong to the Lord. He is the master. Ask God to change your desires. Ask him to help you to choose time with him instead of the extra half-hour in bed, watching TV, household chores, chatting with friends. Remember the foolish virgins. (See Matthew 25:1-14.) They could not light their lamps with someone else's oil. In just the same way no one else can build a relationship with God for you. You must do it yourself. As you come to love and worship Jesus you will not fear his coming. You will gladly welcome it.

DAY 3

(Luke 11:1)
Now it happened that he was in a certain place praying, and when he had finished one of his disciples said, 'Lord, teach us to pray, as John taught his disciples'.

When you hear, in today's reading, that the disciples asked Jesus to teach them to pray, do you suppose that they had never prayed up to that point in their lives? This is highly unlikely. It is more likely that they had read the Scriptures from youth like all Jewish children, that they attended the synagogue on the Sabbath and followed the customary Jewish daily prayer formula.

Why then did they ask Jesus to teach them? Hearing Jesus and watching him pray with such intimacy to his Father in heaven must have puzzled and surprised them. Such intimacy indicated a level of personal relationship that eluded them. Their request, therefore, suggests a new level of humility that lays aside pre-conceived and established patterns of prayer and leaves the heart open to be taught by God. This is what God is calling you to do this Advent.

Beg the Holy Spirit to show you how much you need to be taught, how you need the Spirit's enlightenment to make Scripture come alive. Then you will begin to experience God as your loving Father. You will grasp the reality of his plan of salvation for your life and come to know and accept Jesus as your Saviour. Ultimately, this will lead you to realise that you can become like Jesus in your prayer. Like him, you will desire above all else to give glory to your Father in heaven. 'Hallowed be thy name, thy kingdom come.'

DAY 4

(Luke 10:21-22)
Just at this time, filled with joy by the Holy Spirit, he said, 'I bless you, Father, Lord of heaven and of earth, for hiding these things from the learned and the clever and revealing them to little children. Yes, Father, for that is what it has pleased you to do. Everything has been entrusted to me by my Father; and no one knows who the Son is except the Father, and who the Father is except the Son and those to whom the Son chooses to reveal him.'

When you begin to pray and read Scripture you may feel that it does not seem very relevant. You may even come to the conclusion that it is beyond your grasp; that it is only for the highly educated. This is simply not true. In the time of Jesus the Pharisees were experts in Scripture, they could quote it in every situation, yet it was not these whom Jesus called blessed. In fact he said that because of their pride in their own intellects the real truth was hidden from them.

Instead, Jesus tells us that those who have a childlike mentality are blessed. It is to these that the Father reveals his power and love and glory. Such people recognise the darkness of mind and separation from God that is the result of sin. Do you know that pride, self-centredness and lack of forgiveness prevent you from hearing God speak to you through his Word? As you repent and accept forgiveness you will come to a new understanding of the truth contained in Scripture. How foolish it would be to hold on to a grudge at the expense of losing the assuring touch of God's forgiveness and love.

As you read and study Scripture today, ask the Holy Spirit to show you the obstacles to his grace in your life. Then as you ask God questions, expect that he will answer in a way that will change your life.

DAY 5

(2 Peter 1:19-20)
So we have confirmation of the words of the prophets; and you will be right to pay attention to it as to a lamp for lighting a way through the dark, until the dawn comes and the morning star rises in your minds. At the same time, we must recognise that the interpretation of scriptural prophecy is never a matter for the individual.

Today's Scripture passage makes a reference to finding our way in the dark. In casual conversation we often refer to being 'in the dark' about some matter. This comment means we are not aware of the facts or that the full truth eludes us in some way.

If we are unaware of the basic truths of our faith we are attempting to live our lives in the darkness of ignorance and unbelief. On the other hand, as we daily present to our minds the truth of God's Word our pathway through life is lit up as by a lamp. The psalmist says 'Your word is a lamp for my feet, a light on my path' *(Psalm 119:105).*

Take some time today to look at the basic truths in 'A Structure for Prayer'. It is not sufficient to read the truths. It is necessary to bring a truth prayerfully before the Lord and ask him to touch your mind with his Holy Spirit. Take a truth like 'God created you out of love and loves you always'. Ask God to teach you that he loves you, that there never was and never will be a time in all eternity when he will cease loving you. If you experience doubt, resistance, cynicism or hesitation in relation to this truth ask him to show you the root of this. Bring that obstacle to the foot of the cross of Jesus and ask him to heal you. Repent of unbelief in his faithful love and make a clear decisive stand in accepting his love in faith, no matter what your feelings dictate. 'Lord help me to believe in your love. Take away the unbelief and darkness of my mind.'

DAY 6

(2 Timothy 3:16-17)
All Scripture is inspired by God and useful for refuting error, for guiding people's lives and teaching them to be upright. This is how someone who is dedicated to God becomes fully equipped and ready for any good work.

Sacred Scripture is the Word of God. God in his kindness and goodness so desires to communicate with us that through his Holy Spirit he speaks with his Word in a way that we as humans and as his creatures can understand. One of the early Church Fathers, St John Chrysostom, commenting on this says: 'We can learn the gentle kindness of God, which words cannot express, and how far he has gone in adapting this language with thoughtful concern for our weak human nature.'

In its Document on Revelation, the Second Vatican Council teaches very clearly the sacred origin of the Scriptures: 'They have God as their author and have been handed on as such to the Church herself. In composing the sacred books, God chose men and while employed by him they make use of their powers and abilities so that with him acting in them and through them, they, as true authors, consigned to writing everything and only those things which he wanted' *(Dei Verbum, 11)*.

Take up your Bible today, recognise that it is the Word of God and that through it he will teach, correct, guide and equip you and make you ready for 'every good work'. God's desire is that we come to know him in an intimate way. Scripture is a precious gift from God to enable us to do this. St John stated that the purpose of his Gospel was 'that you may believe that Jesus is the Christ, the Son of God' and that 'you may have life through his name' *(John 20:31)*. Ask the Holy Spirit to convince you of the importance of overcoming any resistance you may experience to reading God's Word. Advent is a time to beg God to reveal himself to you through the words of Scripture. Maybe you could set aside some extra time this week to begin to read one of the Gospels in preparation for the coming of Jesus.

DAY 7

(Isaiah 25:6-8)
On this mountain, for all peoples, the Lord Sabaoth is preparing a banquet of rich food, a banquet of fine wines, of succulent food, of well-strained wines. On this mountain, he has destroyed the veil which used to veil all peoples, the pall enveloping all nations; he has destroyed death for ever. The Lord God has wiped away the tears from every cheek; he has taken his people's shame away everywhere on earth, for the Lord has spoken.

Do you believe that God has your best interests at heart? Perhaps you look at your life and see that it is riddled with fear, disappointment, resentments from the past and vague apprehension about the future. You may blame God and doubt his love for you. Such confusion and pain is not part of God's plan for your life. He wants you to look to him, learn his ways and put your trust in him. Jesus has come as your saviour. As you pray and read Scripture the Holy Spirit will reveal the goodness and mercy of God to you. Our God is a bountiful Father. He longs to show his personal love for all people and to give them the richest of blessings.

Hundreds of years before Jesus came, the prophet Isaiah foretold the amazing spiritual blessing that the Lord had in store for those who put their trust in the promise of a redeemer. Under the symbolism of food he likens it to a great wedding celebration.

Turn to the Lord in faith today and ask him to touch your mind with the truth of his promise. Ask him to show you that all the blessings that were promised are to be found in Jesus, the Messiah. Ask him to fill you with expectation and hope in the coming of your Saviour at Christmas. His provision for your life will be beyond anything you could imagine. As you persevere in establishing a daily prayer time the Word of God will slowly and definitely strengthen your weak faith.

'Father, I am sorry for believing more in my own experience of life than in the truth of your Word. I expect Jesus to come into my life, for he alone can take away that veil that separates me from the certainty of your love. I believe that since you created me out of love your plans for my life are for good and not for evil, to give me a future and a hope. Mary, my Mother, ask your divine Son to quieten my mind so that I can ponder the Word as you did.'

At the end of Week 1
* Review the outline of Presentation 1.

* Review your notes on what God has been teaching you during your daily prayer and Scripture reading.

* Thank God for what he is teaching you.

* Make a resolution to be faithful to daily prayer and Scripture reading during the coming week.

OUTLINE OF PRESENTATION 2:
GOD'S MERCY FOR HIS PEOPLE

THE MESSAGE OF REPENTANCE

John the Baptist preached a message of repentance and forgiveness for sin. (See Mark 1:4.) Jesus preached the same message. (See Mark 1:15.) God intended that all men and women would live in intimate relationship with him. Sin disrupted God's plan. (See Genesis 3:6-7.) The original act of disobedience has affected every man and woman who has lived since that time. (See Romans 5:12.) God's love for us was shown in his decision to send Jesus into the world to redeem us. (See Romans 5:8.) Many people today have lost their 'sense of sin'. They experience an 'interior resistance' to recognising sin. We need to pray that we will recognise clearly the sin in our lives.

KNOWING GOD'S FORGIVENESS

God's desire is not to condemn us but to free us from sin. (See John 3:17.) If we beg God's forgiveness we can be sure we will receive it. (See 1 John 1:8-9.) The Holy Spirit works to enable us to recognise our sin and seek forgiveness. (See John 16:8-11.) There are many people who have rejected God's plan for their lives. They may even blame God or think that he has not answered their prayers. As they recognise their sin they can turn to God in repentance and be forgiven.

HEALING OF RELATIONSHIPS

Frequently, anger, bitterness and resentment can destroy relationships in families and between individuals. Jesus wants to heal these relationships as his Christmas gift to us. We should ask God to show us any hidden anger or resentment we are nursing towards other people. We should repent and pray that we will be able to forgive them. We should go to confession and receive God's forgiveness and healing.

There is a special need for healing within families. Much could be gained by arranging a time of reconciliation in your family. This would include looking at ways in which family members have hurt one another and asking for forgiveness. It would also be an opportunity for family members to re-affirm their love for one another and to resolve to avoid hurtful ways of acting and speaking in the future. (See Ephesians 4:29.)

Through the death and resurrection of Christ we have become 'new creations' *(2 Corinthians 5:17).* St Paul appeals to the Corinthians to be reconciled to God. (See 2 Corinthians 5:20.) This appeal is addressed to us also as we prepare for Christmas.

---

* **During the coming week read over this outline each day.**

* **Look up the Scripture passages listed.**

* **Ask the Holy Spirit to help you to understand what you read.**

DAY 1

(Mark 1:14-15)
After John had been arrested, Jesus went into Galilee. There he proclaimed the gospel from God saying, 'The time is fulfilled, and the kingdom of God is close at hand. Repent, and believe the gospel.'

All through the Old Testament God promised a Messiah, one who would come and restore the relationship with him that had been lost when humankind rebelled against its loving creator. Sin and separation darkened people's minds to the true meaning of this promise. Many had an expectation that the coming of the Messiah would mean restoration and advancement in the political and material sphere. Indeed because we do not grasp the true horror of sin and our need for Jesus Christ as Saviour, we very often look for a God who will primarily improve our earthly existence. How much prayer revolves around our own self-centred concerns?

At the beginning of his preaching Jesus explains the true meaning of his mission — the Kingdom of God is at hand. He calls all men and women to repent. What does it mean to repent? Full repentance means changing those ways of thinking, acting and speaking that are contrary to God's will. Repentance is the inner conversion of a person's mind. Many times in the last week's meditations you were encouraged to read the Word of God. As you continue to do this you will discover the will of God. You will discover your true identity which has been clouded over and disfigured by sin. 'For my thoughts are not your thoughts and your ways are not my ways, declares the Lord'(Isaiah 55:8).

Genuine repentance is a gift of the Holy Spirit which leads us to acknowledge our sins, take responsibility for them and then turn away from our own self-centred attitudes. The final step is to ask and accept forgiveness from our loving Father in heaven.

DAY 2

(Romans 13:11-14)
Besides, you know the time has come; the moment is here for you to stop sleeping and wake up, because by now our salvation is nearer than when we first began to believe. The night is nearly over, daylight is on the way; so let us throw off everything that belongs to the darkness and equip ourselves for the light. Let us live decently, as in the light of day; with no orgies or drunkenness, no promiscuity or licentiousness, and no wrangling or jealousy. Let your armour be the Lord Jesus Christ, and stop worrying about how your disordered natural inclinations may be fulfilled.

Fifteen hundred years ago, this text from the Letter to the Romans so touched the mind of a young self-willed intellectual and man of the world that he was shocked out of his unbelief and sinful pattern of living. Later, appalled at the horror of his sinful past in rejecting the living God, he cried out in a mixture of regret and joy: 'Late have I loved thee oh beauty ever ancient and ever new.' This young man was to be the great teacher of the faith and Bishop of Hippo. For Augustine, it was not too late. He accepted the grace of God that showed him the futility of seeking satisfaction in success, ambition, sinful relationships and pursuit of worldly pleasures.

It is not too late for you either. This Advent, God is allowing you to be aware of the urgency of his call in your life. The day of salvation has come. Jesus Christ has come to save you. This is not the time to dilly-dally with sin. Beg the Holy Spirit to show you your sin so that you will see and appreciate your need of Jesus as saviour. Of course the spirit of the world all around you will consistently convince you that you are all right, that there is no need to take this so seriously. Writing to the Corinthians Paul says: 'If our gospel seems to be veiled at all, it is so to those who are on the way to destruction, the unbelievers whose minds have been blinded by the god of this world, so that they cannot see shining the light of the gospel of the glory of Christ, who is the image of God' *(2 Corinthians 4:3-4)*. Later in the same letter he writes: 'As his fellow-workers, we urge you not to let your acceptance of his grace come to nothing. As he said, ''At the time of my favour I have answered you; on the day of salvation I have helped you'' well, now is the real time of favour, now the day of salvation is here' *(2 Corinthians 6:1-2)*.

DAY 3

(John 16:7-8)
Still, I am telling you the truth: it is for your own good that I am going, because unless I go, the Paraclete will not come to you; but if I go, I will send him to you. And when he comes, he will show the world how wrong it was, about sin, and about who was in the right, and about judgement.

Our reaction to our sinful condition can be a defensiveness that resists the reality of sin altogether. Another reaction can be one of guilt and condemnation, leading to depression and hopelessness. Such a way of thinking indicates a lack of understanding of the basic truths of the Gospel. These include our sinful condition and God's work of salvation through the cross of Jesus and the outpouring of the Holy Spirit. Why not take some time this week to read the story of humankind's rebellion against God in Genesis, Chapter 3. It captures the essence of sin. As you read, ask the Holy Spirit to reveal how each of us now manifests the same attitudes as Adam and Eve.

Let us look at some of the characteristics of sin:

1. Unbelief
Adam and Eve, when confronted by the serpent's refutation of God's command, chose to accept the word of the evil one - which they had no reason to trust - against the Word of God.

2. Independence
Adam and Eve didn't want any restrictions placed on them by God. They thought they could control their lives without further need of him. They rejected God's authority.

3. Emotions over truth
When Adam and Eve were created by God their minds were subject to God's Spirit. Their emotions in turn were subject to their minds. Sin reverses this order and our first parents used their minds to reject God's revelation, accepting the serpent's insinuations and leading them to suspect God. In other words they made their decision based on feelings: 'The fruit looks good.'

4. Deceit and fear
The immediate result of disobedience was fear. They became afraid of God. When Adam was confronted by God he did not give a straight answer but blamed his wife and then blamed God for giving him this companion.

Jesus Christ became man, died and rose again. He promises that the Holy Spirit will convince you of your sin; that he will show how the sin of Adam and Eve is your sin. Pope John Paul II says: 'Thus in this "convincing concerning sin" we discover a double gift: the gift of the truth of conscience and the gift of the certainty of redemption. The Spirit of truth is the Counsellor' *(Dominum et Vivificantem, 31).*

DAY 4

(Ephesians 4:1-3)
I, the prisoner in the Lord, urge you therefore to lead a life worthy of the vocation to which you were called. With all humility and gentleness, and with patience, support each other in love. Take every care to preserve the unity of the Spirit by the peace that binds you together.

God's plan for our lives is that we live in loving relationship with each other. When humankind rejected a relationship with God it seriously damaged its capacity to relate with others. Since the source of life is rejected, humankind, unaided, cannot re-establish friendly relationships. 'Wounded in this way, man almost inevitably causes damage to the fabric of his relationship with others and with the created world. This is... verified in many ways in the human psyche and in the spiritual life, as well as in society, where it is easy to see the signs and effects of internal disorder' *(Reconciliatio et Paenitentia, 15)*.

Advent is a time when God particularly wants to heal broken relationships. Look into your life today and ask the Holy Spirit to show you the root of unforgiveness, self-righteousness, resentment and critical attitudes. These cause division and make it difficult for you to love others. Maybe you experience a level of hopelessness and unbelief that prevents you from having a sense of expectation that God can heal divisions and help you let go of bitterness. The wound of broken human relationships can only be healed if the root infection of sin against God has been dealt with through the cross of Jesus Christ.

In our parish there may be people we do not like, people with whom we find it difficult to be friendly. These may be people who refuse to forgive others; people who nurse grudges against those with whom they have clashed in the past; people whose mannerisms cause irritation. Jesus had strong words to say about such thinking: 'Anyone who is angry with a brother will answer for it before the court; anyone who calls a brother ''Fool'' will answer for it before the Sanhedrin'*(Matthew 5:22)*. It is a sin for someone who has been chosen by God, redeemed by Christ, and is indwelt by the Holy Spirit, to be treated in a negative and scornful way. We must repent and ask forgiveness for the ways in which we do not accept fellow-believers as our family in Christ. Pause for a moment and ask the Holy Spirit to show you those people in your parish or community with whom you are not at peace. Ask for the grace of repentance, tell the Lord you are sorry and be cleansed by the blood of Jesus. Thank God specifically for these individuals (name them now), bring them to the foot of the cross and know that they are loved by God and called to eternal life.

DAY 5

(Ephesians 2:14-16)
For he is the peace between us, and has made the two into one entity and broken down the barrier which used to keep them apart, by destroying in his own person the hostility, that is, the Law of commandments with its decrees. His purpose in this was, by restoring peace, to create a single New Man out of the two of them, and through the cross, to reconcile them both to God in one Body; in his own person he killed the hostility.

'He (Christ) is our peace.' Sometimes when we think of Jesus coming into the world we imagine a helpless, weak infant. What we celebrate during the feast of Christmas is much more than that. It is the celebration of our salvation when Jesus came 'to save his people from their sins' *(Matthew 1:21)*. He comes as the God of peace who proclaims and makes peace through the work of his cross. He puts an end to the enmity between God and humankind. The root of all enmity between human beings is pride. This pride is sin and leads to death. It is only when we come to understand truly the nature of sin that we shall realise the nature of salvation. But we only want the positive. 'Don't worry about the negative, don't talk too much about sin; I only want to know about the love of God.'

In order to measure the love of God you must appreciate the depth of the separation between you and God. By the free choice of our wills we see how we set ourselves up against God and in our pride and self-centredness we make ourselves into rival gods. It might be good to examine your conscience at this point and ask the Holy Spirit to show you your self-interest, self-love and self-praise. Examine your thoughts and see how often they turn on and revolve around self. God ordained that our lives be under his authority and constantly seeking his ways. 'Do not congratulate yourself on your own wisdom, fear the Lord and turn your back on evil' *(Proverbs 3:7)*.

To say Jesus is our peace means that he is the only one who, as both God and man, could stand in our place before God and make atonement for our rebellion.

We believe that in Jesus we have forgiveness of our sins and reconciliation with the Father. Through faith in Jesus' saving death for us, we know that God has forgiven our sins. As we accept this in faith we will see the power of the cross at work in our lives, putting an end to old patterns of sin. In the face of evil, when confronted by temptation, we can pray: 'Behold the cross of Christ. Fly all you powers of darkness; the lion of the tribe of Judah (Jesus) has triumphed' *(St Anthony of Padua)*.

DAY 6

(1 John 1:7-9)
But if we live in light, as he is in light, we have a share in each other's life, and the blood of Jesus, his Son, cleanses us from all sin. If we say, 'We have no sin,' we are deceiving ourselves, and truth has no place in us; if we acknowledge our sins, he is trustworthy and upright, so that he will forgive our sins and will cleanse us from all evil.

God's promises were fulfilled when Jesus came. We need no longer live in darkness and confusion. Be full of expectation that as you are faithful to prayer, repentance and reading of the Scriptures, God will bring you into his wonderful light. Pray that this Christmas, as you light your windows with the Christmas candle, it will not be an empty symbol. Your lives and homes will be lit by a new realisation of the presence and power of Jesus.

Why is Christ our light? He is our light because by the shedding of his blood he has taken us out of the darkness of our sin. Because of this perfect cleansing we can draw near to God. The blood of Jesus tells you that your sin is forgiven, you are no longer guilty, you are no longer in disgrace and shame before God. You have been made a child of God. Jesus has taken the punishment; he has borne the sin; he has paid by his death so that you might live forever. 'We have then, brothers, complete confidence through the blood of Jesus in entering the sanctuary, by a new way which he has opened for us....So as we go in, let us be sincere in heart and filled with faith, our hearts sprinkled and free from any trace of bad conscience' *(Hebrews 10:19-22).*

Why not begin today to pray about your preparation for confession? In confession we kneel before Christ and with grateful hearts acknowledge that by his wounds we have been healed. In our weakness and sinful state we come. With the assurance of faith, we find deliverance from our sin. In preparation we need to pray that the Holy Spirit will enlighten our minds and convince us of our sins. The hidden and deceptive roots of sin must be touched by the cross of Christ. 'But who can detect his own failings? Wash away my hidden faults, and from pride preserve your servant. Never let it be my master' *(Psalm 19:12-13).*

A good confession brings God's peace. It is described by John Paul II as 'A celebration in the very depths of self and thus a regaining of lost joy, the joy of being saved, which the majority of people in our times are no longer capable of experiencing' *(Reconciliatio et Paenitentia, 31).* We can stand before God in the assurance that we are free and totally accepted by our heavenly Father as his children. 'Thus condemnation will never come to those who are in Christ Jesus' *(Romans 8:1).*

DAY 7

(1 Peter 1:18-21)
For you know that the price of your ransom from the futile way of life handed down from your ancestors was paid, not in anything perishable like silver or gold, but in precious blood as of a blameless and spotless lamb, Christ. He was marked out before the world was made, and was revealed at the final point of time for your sake. Through him you now have faith in God, who raised him from the dead and gave him glory for this very purpose - that your faith and hope should be in God.

In his letter to these newly baptised Christians Peter encouraged them to realise the gift they have received. When we are baptised we are given a new life. The blood of Jesus has paid the penalty for our old sinful life that leads only to death. This new life is a pledge of our eternal inheritance in heaven. As baptised Christians we all have the seed of this new life. Due to lack of understanding and failure to pray and study the Word of God, many Christians do not experience the reality. This might be a good time to reflect on how well you have studied the weekly teachings you have been receiving in the Advent programme.

It is only as the basic gospel truths replace the futile patterns of thinking in our own minds that we will see changes in our lives. 'For all humanity is grass, and all its beauty like the wild flower's.... The grass withers, the flower fades, but the word of the Lord remains for ever' *(Isaiah 40:6-8)*.

What do we mean by 'the futile way of life'? The dictionary defines futile as worthless, useless, unavailing and ineffectual. Such a way of life flows from a mind that is unrenewed by the Holy Spirit. Satan constantly works in our minds to turn them away from God's plan for our lives. St Paul urged the Christians of Ephesus not to go on 'living the empty-headed life that the gentiles do' *(Ephesians 4:17)*. He understood the root of sinful behaviour was to be found in wrong patterns of thinking in people's minds. Such thinking leads one to doubt one's reason for living and leads to frustration. Life becomes a ceaseless effort to fill a void with an endless round of experiences and ambitions.

In Christ, we have access to his wisdom and power. While living in the world it is possible to live and work on a spiritual plane as well. We are able to use our minds to see and destroy false attitudes and the prejudices of our fallen nature. Christians should be alert to what would be thought, said, and done in Christ: 'Do not model your behaviour on the contemporary world, but let the renewing of your minds transform you so that you can discern for yourselves what is the will of God' *(Romans 12:2)*.

At the end of Week 2

* **Review the outline of Presentation 2.**

* **Make a resolution to be faithful to daily prayer and Scripture reading during the coming week.**

OUTLINE OF PRESENTATION 3:
THE PROMISE OF A SAVIOUR

After the Fall human beings were in a tragic condition and their situation looked hopeless. Immediately God showed his mercy by promising to send a Saviour. (See Genesis 3:15.) Through the centuries this promise was renewed and clarified many times.

ABRAHAM, OUR FATHER IN FAITH
God chose Abraham to be the leader of a new people. He made an agreement with him and promised to remain with him and his descendants forever. (See Genesis 17:5-8.) This promise was repeated to David, who was assured that one of his sons would be a king. (See 1 Chronicles 17:14.) Later it became clear that a child would be born in Bethlehem. He would be a descendant of David and his throne would be secure and would last for ever. (See Isaiah 9:5-6; Micah 5:2.) This child would be the Messiah. He would be without sin but he would suffer and die for the sins of all people. (See Isaiah 53:4-5.) Through his sufferings he would break the power of sin and evil. This is what was actually accomplished by Jesus when he came. (See Matthew 1:21; John 1:29.) He took away the sins of the world. People today need to look to Jesus to be freed of their sins. Any other solution will not bring lasting peace of mind.

PREPARING FOR THE SAVIOUR
One way to see how we can prepare for Christmas is to consider the example of Zechariah, the father of John the Baptist. When he was told that his wife would give birth to a child his reaction was one of disbelief. (See Luke 1:5-25.) Yet when the time came for the baby to be born he was able to be obedient to God. (See Luke 1:63-64.) It is likely that he used the intervening time to meditate on the promises of God in the Old Testament. (See Luke 1:68-69.) Zechariah understood that John the Baptist's role was to bring people forgiveness of their sins. (See Luke 1:77.) God's promises came alive for him and his faith grew stronger. The Holy Spirit enlightened his mind and his faith became a living faith.

THE FULFILMENT
Jesus claimed that he was the fulfilment of the promises made in the Old Testament. (See Luke 24:25-27.) He reminded his disciples that his death was necessary 'to save his people from their sins'. You can expect that you, too, will be freed from sin as you celebrate the birth of Jesus this Christmas.

---

* During the coming week read over this outline each day.

* Look up the Scripture passages listed.

* Ask the Holy Spirit to help you to understand what you read.

DAY 1

(James 5:7-10)
Now be patient, brothers, until the Lord's coming. Think of a farmer: how patiently he waits for the precious fruit of the ground until it has had the autumn rains and the spring rains! You too must be patient; do not lose heart, because the Lord's coming will be soon. Do not make complaints against one another, brothers, so as not to be brought to judgement yourselves; the Judge is already to be seen waiting at the gates. For your example, brothers, in patiently putting up with persecution, take the prophets who spoke in the Lord's name.

Have you ever wondered why people who appear to be dishonest and unjust often get on well in life? Sometimes those who are rich seem to be successful in everything. St James speaks about the question in the section of his letter preceding that given above. (See James 5:1-6.) He says: 'On earth you have had a life of comfort and luxury; in the time of slaughter you went on eating to your heart's content' *(V.5)*. But he also says: 'Your wealth is rotting....All your gold and your silver are corroding away....' *(V.1-3)*. Then in the section given above he addresses those who are suffering because of their faith in God: 'Now be patient, brothers, until the Lord's coming' *(V.7)*. Wasn't this a strange way to speak to those who were in distress? St James did not regard it as strange because he knew the truth of God. He knew the promises God had made to his people through the Old Testament prophets *(V.10)*. He knew that the promises of God are everlasting: 'The grass withers, the flower fades, but the word of the Lord remains for ever' *(Isaiah 40:8)*.

At Christmas we celebrate the first coming of Jesus into the world. We know that Jesus will come again (second coming) and that he will reward those who have been faithful to him in this world. Do you display the kind of patience that is spoken about by St James or are you overwhelmed by the circumstances of your life? This Christmas, you can expect Jesus to reveal himself to you in a personal way. This will bring a change in your life and give glory to God. In your prayer today profess your faith in God and in the promises he has made to you. Say: 'Lord, I believe in your faithfulness and love. I believe that you have a plan for my life. I know that you will never abandon me.' As you do this, you can expect to experience peace and joy, even in the face of difficulties and disappointments.

DAY 2

(2 Peter 3:8-9)
But there is one thing, my dear friends, that you must never forget: that with the Lord, a day is like a thousand years, and a thousand years are like a day. The Lord is not being slow in carrying out his promises, as some people think he is; rather is he being patient with you, wanting nobody to be lost and everybody to be brought to repentance.

St Peter was concerned that his readers should be living holy and saintly lives. (See 2 Peter 3:11.) He understood that God had given them the gift of repentance so that they could be constantly receiving God's forgiveness. Do you look on repentance as a gift from God? Most people look on it as something unpleasant and try to avoid it. The truth is that we don't want to admit that we have deliberately done wrong. We become defensive and make excuses. But if we are honest we must admit that we sin deliberately and do so frequently.

Paul did not regard repentance as a hardship imposed on us by an angry God. Rather, he understood it as a response to God's kindness. He asked the Romans: 'Do you not know that God's kindness is meant to lead you to repentance?' *(Romans 2:4)*. Paul knew that repentance is an expression of the Father's kindness because he understood that repentance brings life. Without repentance we could not escape condemnation and guilt. God invites us to realise that repentance is a precious gift. Through it we are freed of the burden of sin and guilt. Our minds are freed to understand the Scriptures and we desire to praise and thank God. Each time we recognise sin in our lives we can turn to God and repent. As we do we are assured of God's forgiveness. Let us approach God each day, aware of our sinful state and confident of his mercy.

DAY 3

(Romans 1:18-23)
The retribution of God from heaven is being revealed against the ungodliness and injustice of human beings who in their injustice hold back the truth. For what can be known about God is perfectly plain to them, since God has made it plain to them: ever since the creation of the world, the invisible existence of God and his everlasting power have been clearly seen by the mind's understanding of created things. And so these people have no excuse: they knew God and yet they did not honour him as God or give thanks to him, but their arguments became futile and their uncomprehending minds were darkened. While they claimed to be wise, in fact they were growing so stupid that they exchanged the glory of the immortal God for an imitation, for the image of a mortal human being, or of birds, or animals, or crawling things.

It is very easy to approach the celebration of Christmas as if we did not need the coming of Jesus. When we read carefully the above passage from St Paul's letter to the Romans we can see that it is a description of the state of human beings after the Fall. Does this sound exaggerated to you? It is important to ask the Holy Spirit to help you to understand the truth of these words. They make clear to us that we need Jesus to come as Saviour and redeemer. Without the coming of Jesus and his death and resurrection men and women would be separated from God and could never enter into relationship with him. Men and women had turned away from God so radically that the death of the Son of God was necessary so as to restore the relationship.

What was true of men and women in the first century is equally true of each one of us today. We start off life separated from God in the same way as they did. Only the death and resurrection of Jesus can restore us to that relationship. We can make the mistake of thinking that we only need the power of Jesus when we are in trouble. Then when the crisis passes we feel confident that we can live our lives independently of God. We can treat Jesus in the same way as we treat medicine prescribed by the doctor. If we take medicine and it is successful we don't need it any longer. Jesus wants us to know that he is the Lord of heaven and earth. He loves us and watches over us every day. He wants us to know that we need him every moment to enable us to live in relationship with God. As you prepare to celebrate Christmas, ask the Holy Spirit to enable you to understand how much you need the coming of Jesus. Speak to him in your prayer and profess your faith in him and in his love for you. Admit your need of him and invite him to come to you and change your life this Christmas.

DAY 4

(Luke 1:5-6)
In the days of King Herod of Judaea there lived a priest called Zechariah who belonged to the Abijah section of the priesthood, and he had a wife, Elizabeth by name, who was a descendant of Aaron. Both were upright in the sight of God and impeccably carried out all the commandments and observances of the Lord. But they were childless: Elizabeth was barren and they were both advanced in years.

How did John the Baptist develop the character that made him so remarkable in his ability to obey God and preach his Word? It is clear that the upbringing he received in his home prepared him to receive this grace from God. St Luke tells us that Zechariah and Elizabeth were 'upright in the sight of God and impeccably carried out all the commandments and observances of the Lord' *(V.6)*. Like the parents of today, the difficulties they faced in bringing their children to God were enormous. But they had learned how to depend on the power of the Holy Spirit. Here is the witness of a young father who discovered this, also:

> Even though we were living together and had three children, I hardly ever communicated with my wife. We didn't see eye to eye on many things so that much of what started out as communication ended up as arguments. As far as disciplining the children was concerned, I left it to my wife. I really wasn't sure enough of myself to do it. As a result, she was burdened almost entirely with the job of rearing them.
>
> Then, a few years ago, I learned about God's desire to transform those who believe in him and who call upon the Holy Spirit as their own source of power. It now seems unbelievable to me when I look back and see how much my life and the lives of my wife and children have changed since then. I learned how to pray, how to come into God's presence, praise him, listen to him and communicate to him directly and honestly all my fears, anxieties and problems. Out of this prayer, things began to change.
>
> A few years ago, differences of opinion would have made me ready to call it quits; separation seemed almost inevitable. But God has become the basis of my marriage and both my wife and I have started praying, sometimes together. We can and do discuss even the most difficult subjects, ones which we would go to great lengths to avoid in the past. Not only do we discuss them, we resolve them. The Lord has really worked in our lives.

This Advent God is prepared to pour out these blessings on all people — whether married or single, priest or religious. He will give you the strength and courage to witness to the truths of the life and death of Christ to your family and friends, your parishioners or those you serve. Ask the Holy Spirit to give you his gifts so that you can understand and proclaim the Good News of Jesus Christ.

DAY 5

(Romans 5:6-8)
When we were still helpless, at the appointed time, Christ died for the godless. You could hardly find anyone ready to die even for someone upright; though it is just possible that, for a really good person, someone might undertake to die. So it is proof of God's own love for us, that Christ died for us while we were still sinners.

There are many conflicting ideas about the meaning of love in the world today. A glance at a good dictionary will show the wide variety of meanings for this word. Most of these meanings refer to how men and women relate with one another. According to Scripture the word refers, first of all, to God's love for us: 'Love consists in this: it is not we who loved God, but God loved us and sent his Son to expiate our sins' *(1 John 4:10)*. St Paul tells us, in the passage above, that the death of Christ is a proof of God's love for us.

God's love for us does not stop there. God's concern for us means that he sees our weakness and confusion. This is the same love that Jesus showed for the crowds who followed him while he was on earth. 'So as he stepped ashore he saw a large crowd; and he took pity on them because they were like sheep without a shepherd' *(Mark 6:34)*. Jesus was concerned at the fact that they had no food and were hungry. But he was even more concerned about their spiritual poverty, i.e. that they did not know the truth of God: 'and he set himself to teach them at some length' *(Mark 6:34)*. Jesus is concerned about that same poverty in the lives of Christians today. How can you ensure that you can avail of the rich food that Jesus provides for you? One way is to take part faithfully in the Advent Programme and to study the points that are dealt with in the weekly meeting. A very important part of the programme is being faithful to daily prayer and Scripture reading. In your daily prayer you should pay special attention to repeating the truths contained in the Creed or going over the basic facts and reading the Scripture passages given in the Structure for Prayer. Ask yourself as you read: Who is God? Ask the Holy Spirit to reveal his glory and majesty to you. He is the magnificent master of the universe. 'Yours, oh Lord, is the greatness, the power, the splendour, length of days and glory, everything in heaven and on earth is yours' *(1 Chronicles 29:11)*. Every time you profess your faith in these truths they become established more firmly in your mind. This brings a greater clarity about the truth of God's love for you. Finally, you can help your family to prepare for the celebration of Christmas by involving them in some of the activities for families suggested in this handbook.

DAY 6

(John 1:1-3)
In the beginning was the Word: the Word was with God and the Word was God. He was with God in the beginning. Through him all things came into being, not one thing came into being except through him.

The opening section from John's Gospel can make an extraordinary impact on our minds as we read it. Throughout his Gospel John tries to communicate to his readers the greatness and majesty of Jesus. He does this in a special way in the opening section which is called the 'Prologue'. John had a clear grasp of the fact that Jesus did not begin to exist when he was born in Bethlehem. He existed from all eternity: 'He was with God in the beginning' *(V.2)*. He existed in perfect love and unity with his Father. Jesus was equal to God in every way, yet he became fully man. In obedience to his Father's will he became a man, like us in all things but sin. 'For the high priest we have is not incapable of feeling our weaknesses with us, but has been put to the test in exactly the same way as ourselves, apart from sin' *(Hebrews 4:15)*. Ask the Holy Spirit to give you a clear grasp of this great mystery — that Jesus was fully God and fully man. Ask him to teach you what it means to say that Jesus existed from all eternity and was perfectly united with the Father.

Jesus was the Word of God, who came to bring the message of salvation to humankind. It was clear that even among the chosen people there was opposition to the message of Jesus. 'He came to his own and his own people did not accept him' *(John 1:11)*. Later in the same Gospel Jesus highlighted this opposition when he said: 'In all truth I tell you, we speak about what we know and witness only to what we have seen and yet you people reject our evidence' *(John 3:11)*. This situation has not changed since the time of Jesus. Unbelief is widespread in the world today. In our own lives we find areas in which we resist or even reject the truth of Jesus. One of the results of the Fall is that it causes a darkness of the human mind. We all share this condition because we all share in the sin of Adam and Eve. This makes it difficult to recognise the greatness and majesty of Jesus and the fact that he existed from all eternity. It also causes us to doubt or resist the truth that Jesus has taught us. Jesus promised that the Holy Spirit, whom he would send, would teach his disciples 'everything'. (See John 14:26.) Beg the Holy Spirit to come to you and teach you the truth. If you find resistance to the truth of God within yourself, turn to God and repent. Then beg to be freed of this so that you can believe.

DAY 7

(Luke 8:19-21)
His mother and his brothers came looking for him, but they could not get to him because of the crowd. He was told, 'Your mother and brothers are standing outside and want to see you.' But he said in answer, 'My mother and my brothers are those who hear the word of God and put it into practice.'

At first sight these words of Jesus seem surprising. They almost appear to be a slight on his mother and his closest relatives. It is clear from other statements of Jesus in the Gospels that this was not the case. In fact, what Jesus wanted was to highlight the importance of being in proper spiritual relationship with him. What does this mean? It means listening to and studying the Word of God, as Mary did. (See Luke 2:51.) The Letter to the Hebrews tells us that: 'The word of God is something alive and active: it cuts more incisively than any two-edged sword: it can seek out the place where soul is divided from spirit, or joints from marrow; it can pass judgement on secret emotions and thoughts' *(Hebrews 4:12)*. St Paul says: 'Let the Word of Christ in all its richness find a home with you' *(Colossians 3:16)*.

It is the wish of the Church that every member should pay heed to this advice. When the bishops of the whole world met in Rome for the Second Vatican Council they gave very clear directions to all Catholics: 'Likewise, the sacred Synod forcefully and specifically exhorts all the Christian faithful...to learn ''the surpassing knowledge of Jesus Christ'' (Philippians 3:8) by frequent reading of the divine Scriptures. ''Ignorance of the Scriptures is ignorance of Christ'' (St Jerome). Therefore, let them go gladly to the sacred text itself, whether in the sacred liturgy...or in devout reading, or in such suitable exercises and various other helps which...are happily spreading everywhere in our day' *(Dei Verbum, 25)*.

This is an opportunity for everybody to ask themselves some questions. How much attention do I give to the reading of Scripture? Do I have a good readable copy of the Bible? Do I set time aside each day to read and study the Bible? Do I use suitable aids to help me to get a deeper understanding of the Word of God? Perhaps you did not realise the importance of Scripture in the life of each Christian. If so, you now have an opportunity to set this right. You may need to plan some time when you can regularly read and study the Bible. If you don't have a good modern translation of the Bible you will need to get one. You may also like to get one of the aids that are available to help you in your reading and study. An excellent one is the magazine 'The Word Among Us' which is published every month. (See Family Activities for Advent, p. 44).

At the end of Week 3
* **Review the outline of Presentation 3.**

* **Make a resolution to be faithful to daily prayer and Scripture reading.**

OUTLINE OF PRESENTATION 4:
JESUS, THE FULFILMENT OF THE PROMISE

Jesus is the fulfilment of all the promises made in the Old Testament. In reality, he is more wonderful than the Old Testament prophets could ever have imagined. The New Testament tells us that Jesus 'bears the impress of God's own being' *(Hebrews 1:3)*; that 'he is the image of the unseen God' *(Colossians 1:15)*. It is usual first to recognise Jesus as Saviour - the one who frees us from sin and removes our guilt. However, as we grow spiritually, we will recognise that Jesus is also our Lord and that he is the second person of the Trinity. The truth about Jesus is inexhaustible. There is no limit to the possibilities for growth.

KNOWING THE LOVE OF JESUS
St Paul prayed that the Christians of Ephesus would come to a deeper understanding of the love of Christ. (See Ephesians 3:16-19.) To know Jesus Christ is to know how much love is in his heart for every human being, including every sinner in the world. It includes knowing that he died on the cross to free us from sin. Jesus' love for us is so great that we can never exhaust it or know it fully.

JESUS: THE FULL STORY
The purpose of our lives is to come to a deeper knowledge of Jesus. At Christmas the Church invites us to devote ourselves to prayer and the study of the Word of God. We are invited to reflect more deeply on the truths contained in the Creed. These are also the truths we call to mind in 'A Structure for Prayer'. By accepting this invitation we will come to a deeper knowledge of Jesus.

THE HOLY SPIRIT REVEALS JESUS
The Holy Spirit was sent into the world to make Jesus known as Lord and Saviour and to guide us to the truth. (See John 16:13-14.) Pray each day that the Holy Spirit will reveal Jesus, the faithful Son of the Father, to you, as your Lord and Saviour. Why not continue to pray and read Scripture daily when Advent is over? Try to seek help and support to encourage you to persevere.

---

* **During the coming week read over this outline each day.**

* **Look up the Scripture passages listed.**

* **Ask the Holy Spirit to help you to understand what you read.**

DAY 1

(1 Peter 1:10-11)
This salvation was the subject of the search and investigation of the prophets who spoke of the grace you were to receive, searching out the time and circumstances for which the Spirit of Christ, bearing witness in them, was revealing the sufferings of Christ and the glories to follow them.

All Scripture, Old and New Testament, points to the central reality of the life, death and resurrection of Jesus Christ. These are the events by which we were saved from the effects of the Fall and made children of God. It is not intended that we focus on one aspect of the life of Jesus in isolation from the rest. While we celebrate the birth of Jesus at Christmas it is important not to consider it separately from the rest of his life. In an earlier meditation we saw that Jesus existed from all eternity. In the Gospels we read the story of the life and teaching of Jesus and his death and resurrection.

There is a tendency to focus on the birth of Jesus at Christmas and to lose sight of the reason why he came. This can lead to a sentimental approach to the feast of Christmas. Are you more excited by the thought of a baby in a manger than you are by what Jesus achieved through his death and resurrection? The prophets foretold the sufferings of Christ and the glories that were to follow them. Through the action of the Holy Spirit they understood the condition of the world before Christ came. They drew attention to the tragic consequences of godlessness - sin, guilt, shame and bondage. They never lost sight of the promise of salvation. Often they were unclear as to how this would come about. Yet their faith was unshaken in the certainty of a Saviour: 'But I shall look to the Lord, my hope is in the God who will save me; my God will hear me' *(Micah 7:7)*.

God's love was greater than anything they could imagine. He sent his Son to suffer and die so that the bondage of sin could be broken. 'He was bearing our sins in his own body on the cross, so that we might die to our sins and live for uprightness' *(1 Peter 2:24)*. We can be confident that every sin that has ever been or will ever be committed has been dealt with by the death of Jesus. So too have the effects of sin in our lives. In spite of this we can allow memories of past sins to undermine our relationship with God. Shame, guilt and insecurity can plague us long after sins have been confessed and forgiven. God wants to give us an assurance that all these memories can be healed. During Advent we can turn to Jesus with great expectancy. We can be freed from all the burdens of our past sins. This is the promise of God to his sons and daughters. Beg the Holy Spirit to show you areas where you need healing. Then turn to Jesus with great confidence and invite him to heal you and give you peace.

DAY 2

(Luke 1:67-75)

His father Zechariah was filled with the Holy Spirit and spoke this prophecy: Blessed be the Lord, the God of Israel, for he has visited his people, he has set them free, and he has established for us a saving power in the House of his servant David, just as he proclaimed, by the mouth of his holy prophets from ancient times, that he would save us from our enemies and from the hands of all those who hate us, and show faithful love to our ancestors, and so keep in mind his holy covenant. This was the oath he swore to our father Abraham, that he would grant us, free from fear, to be delivered from the hands of our enemies, to serve him in holiness and uprightness in his presence, all our days.

Advent is a time when God wants to give us a deeper gift of faith. The example of Zechariah can teach us much about how our faith grows. Earlier in St Luke's Gospel we read about the angel's visit to Zechariah to announce the birth of John the Baptist. (See Luke 1:5-25.) At this time Zechariah's faith was weak and he could not believe the message of the angel. As a result he was unable to speak until the baby was born. (See Luke 1:19-20.) At the time of the birth of John the Baptist Zechariah's faith had grown stronger and he was able to be obedient to the message of the angel. Despite the opposition of his relatives and friends he said: '"His name is John." And they were all astonished. At that instant his power of speech returned and he spoke and praised God' *(Luke 1:63-64).*

What happened during those nine months of Elizabeth's pregnancy to transform his mind? It seems likely that he spent much of the time meditating on the promises of God in the Old Testament. In his canticle he praised God, who had established a 'saving power...just as he proclaimed, by the mouth of his holy prophets from ancient times' *(Luke 1:68-69).* Of course he would have known the words of the prophets before the first visit of the angel. He was a priest and, therefore, was familiar with the Scriptures. But it appears that God's promises must not have been alive for him so that his faith was weak. It is likely too that, while he was unable to speak, he would have meditated deeply on the words of the prophets. And as he did, the Holy Spirit would have enlightened his mind, enabling his faith to become a living faith.

We can learn from the example of Zechariah. Do we find that our faith is weak or that we do not have a living knowledge of God? If we are willing to spend time studying and meditating on the words of Scripture we can expect that the Holy Spirit will bring our faith alive and give us a living knowledge of God.

DAY 3

(Galatians 4:4-5)
But when the completion of the time came, God sent his Son, born of a woman, born a subject of the Law, to redeem the subjects of the Law, so that we could receive adoption as sons.

A sad fact today is that many Christians do not have a clear understanding of why Jesus came into the world. Many people think that it was good for Jesus to come but fail to grasp how necessary his coming was. Jesus rebuked the disciples on the road to Emmaus saying: 'You foolish men! So slow to believe all that the prophets have said! Was it not necessary that the Christ should suffer before entering into his glory?' *(Luke 24:25-26)*. It is good to ask in prayer, 'Lord Jesus, why did you become man? Why did you suffer and die?' As you recall the basic truths ask the Holy Spirit to enlighten your mind.

We know that God created the world and everything in it. He created us to live in intimate relationship with himself. He explained the conditions under which we would be able to continue in that relationship. We are familiar with how humankind responded to God's generosity. They refused to believe God's Word and disobeyed him. Therefore, they could no longer experience the intimate personal relationship of being children of God and sharing his glory. Only God himself could restore this relationship. Unfortunately they were not ready for the restoration of their relationship with God immediately. Their minds were so darkened by the Fall that they would not be able to recognise a Saviour if he came among them. God had to begin his work of preparation that would continue for centuries. He chose Abraham to be the father of a new people. God's desire for this people was that they would be holy: 'Be holy, for I, the Lord your God, am holy' *(Leviticus 19:2)*.

This was a long and painful process, as we see from the story of God's people in the Old Testament. When God speaks about the 'completion of the time' he is referring to the conclusion of this long time of preparation for the coming of the Saviour. Jesus longs to act in our lives this Christmas. When Christmas is over you can expect to know that something has changed in your life. God wants this Christmas to be different for you. God's desire for his people is still the same - that they be holy. We can prepare ourselves for God's action by being faithful to daily prayer and Scripture reading and by repenting and asking God's forgiveness for our stubbornness and hardheartedness.

DAY 4

(Matthew 6:31-33)
So do not worry; do not say, 'What are we to eat? What are we to drink? What are we to wear?'
It is the gentiles who set their hearts on all these things. Your heavenly Father knows you need
them all. Set your hearts on his kingdom first, and on God's saving justice, and all these other
things will be given you as well.

Is it possible to avoid anxiety and worry in the time leading up to Christmas? Undoubtedly, there is a lot of pressure in the weeks leading up to Christmas. There is shopping and baking to be done, Christmas presents to be bought, and Christmas cards to be written. There is also the inevitable financial worry associated with this time of year. How can you remain calm and peaceful through all this? You can only do so by being clear in your mind about the real meaning of Christmas.

Christmas is first and foremost a spiritual event - the birth of Jesus, the Son of God, into the world. Jesus tells us to 'set our hearts on his kingdom first' *(V.33)*. One way to do this is by reading and studying the Word of God and asking God to enable you to understand what he wants to teach you. It is important to expect that your prayer will be answered. God loves you deeply and wants to teach you more about himself. As you pray today, ask God to make clear to you the importance of your spiritual preparation for Christmas. This will bring you peace and calm. Material preparations are secondary but they do tend to cause anxiety and worry.

Parents need to ensure that their children are preparing in a prayerful way for the celebration of Christmas. A good way to involve the family is to consider the selection of activities listed at the end of this handbook. Try to use at least one activity that will involve the children in reading Scripture and discussing what God is teaching them through it. A good time to do this might be when the family get together for the evening meal. You could use the Scripture passages and meditations from this booklet or from *The Word Among Us*. You could also try to say together traditional prayers such as the Angelus and Grace before and after Meals. All these are ways in which you can teach your children to 'set their hearts on his kingdom first'. Those who heed the words of Jesus will not be disappointed and will experience great blessings.

DAY 5

(Luke 1:35-36)
The angel answered, 'The Holy Spirit will come upon you, and the power of the Most High will cover you with its shadow. And so the child will be holy and will be called Son of God.'

The birth of Jesus Christ was the result of the action of God. The angel said to Mary: 'The Holy Spirit will come upon you' *(V.35)*. We see how intimately the Holy Spirit was involved in the work of our redemption. Before his death Jesus promised that he would send the Holy Spirit on the apostles. (See John 14:16-17,26; 16:7.) In the Acts of the Apostles we read how closely the Holy Spirit was involved in the growth of the Church. But the activity of the Holy Spirit did not end there. The Holy Spirit has been active in the lives of individuals and groups in every generation. His activity can be seen in the lives of many groups and individuals in the world today. When Jesus promised to send the Holy Spirit he made it clear that one of his primary roles would be to teach the truth to those who would be open to his message. 'When the Spirit of truth comes he will lead you to the complete truth, since he will not be speaking of his own accord but will say only what he has been told' *(John 16:13)*.

Today there is confusion about the truth that Jesus taught. Many people do not understand the purpose for which they have been created or the destiny that God has intended for them. Others do not accept the reality of the Fall and the fact that Jesus needed to die to redeem them. There is widespread confusion about issues of morality, as many Christians base their beliefs on ideas that come from the world around them rather than the gospel.

How can you discover the truth of Jesus in the midst of such conflicting ideas? Remember that it is the role of the Holy Spirit to teach you the truth. As you read Scripture invoke the Holy Spirit to enlighten your mind so that you can understand the truth of what you read. Pray for the grace to be obedient to that truth. One of the truths we learn is that we are children and heirs of God. Because of this fact we have rights and privileges, including the right to receive the gifts of the Spirit that are promised - gifts of wisdom, insight, counsel, power, knowledge and fear of the Lord. (See Isaiah 11:2-3.) These gifts are given to enable us to know God's plan and purpose for our lives. The gifts of the Spirit give us clarity in the ordinary situations of life - to fathers and mothers to be able to care for their children; to employers and employees to enable them to be good stewards of what God has given them; to priests and religious to enable them to care for those who are entrusted into their care. Pray today that you will consciously invite the Holy Spirit into your life and that you will seek his wisdom in the daily situations that arise.

DAY 6

(Luke 1:46-50)
And Mary said: 'My soul proclaims the greatness of the Lord and my spirit rejoices in God my Saviour; because he has looked upon the humiliation of his servant. Yes, from now onwards all generations will call me blessed, for the Almighty has done great things for me. Holy is his name, and his faithful love extends age after age to those who fear him.'

It is unlikely that the words of the Magnificat would have come from Mary's lips if she had not learned to praise and thank God from her childhood. We know that the psalms would have been part of her daily prayer. For example, she would have been accustomed to repeating frequently these words: 'Give thanks to the Lord for he is good, for his faithful love endures for ever' *(Psalm 118:1)*. For modern men and women it is not easy to praise God. Today there is a lot of emphasis on self-fulfilment. People are concerned about their own image, their own success and achievements. These are the drives of the old nature.

But we have become 'new creations' through our faith in Jesus Christ. (See 2 Corinthians 5:17.) As new creations we are called to turn aside from worship of self to praise and worship of God, our creator. St Paul describes very vividly the difference between living according to the old way of life and living as a new creation. (See Ephesians 4:17-32.) For Paul, a key to this new way of living lay in the renewal of the mind. 'Your mind was to be renewed in spirit' *(Ephesians 4:23)*. For us this is equally important. Many of our ideas and patterns of thinking have been formed by the world around us. God's desire is that our minds be renewed and that they be formed by the truth of the gospel. A basic truth is that we have been created by God and depend on him. God is so much greater than we are but he has shown his love for us by making us his sons and daughters. How can we ever thank God enough for such wonderful love? An Old Testament writer expressed clearly what attitude to adopt towards God: 'Exalt the Lord in your praises as high as you may - still he surpasses you' *(Ecclesiasticus 43:30)*.

In his encyclical on Mary, Mother of the Redeemer, Pope John Paul II spoke about Mary's prayer of thanksgiving: 'In the act of creation God gives existence to all that is. In creating man, God gives him the dignity of the image and likeness of himself in a special way as compared with all earthly creatures. Moreover, in his desire to give, God gives himself in the Son, notwithstanding man's sin: "He so loved the world that he gave his only Son" (John 3:16). Mary is the first witness of this marvellous truth, which will be fully accomplished through "the works and words" (Acts 1:1) of her Son and definitively through his Cross and Resurrection' *(Mary, Mother of the Redeemer, 37)*. Pray that you will learn to acknowledge God's greatness as Mary did. Make a decision to read Scripture frequently, especially the Psalms, so that God can teach you how to praise him. Be sure that you devote part of your prayer time every day to praising and thanking God. (See 'A Structure for Prayer' - no.4.) As you do, God will teach you more about his greatness and majesty.

DAY 7

(Hebrews 1:1-3)
At many moments in the past and by many means, God spoke to our ancestors through the prophets;
but in our time, the final days, he has spoken to us in the person of his Son, whom he appointed
heir of all things and through whom he made the ages. He is the reflection of God's glory and
bears the impress of God's own being, sustaining all things by his powerful command; and now
that he has purged sins away, he has taken his seat at the right hand of the divine Majesty on high.

Many Christians today think of God as being 'up there' and distant. What a tragedy this is when we consider the words about Jesus in today's reading: 'He is the reflection of God's glory and bears the impress of God's own being, sustaining all things by his powerful command.' We must keep the two aspects of Jesus clearly in view - his nearness to us in his humanity and the greatness and majesty of his divinity. In 1985 Pope John Paul II spoke about God's nearness to us through his Son: 'God has given the greatest testimony of his nearness by sending on earth his Word, the second person of the Most Holy Trinity, who took on a body like ours and came to live among us.' At the same time we must not forget the greatness and majesty of Jesus. As risen Lord he has been exalted at the right hand of the Father and has been given a name that is above all other names. (See Philippians 2:9.) With what reverence and awe we should come into the presence of God and acknowledge his holiness. We should tremble at the thought of approaching such holiness. And yet this holy God has drawn near to us: 'I dwell in the high and holy place, and also with him who is of a contrite and humble spirit, to revive the spirit of the humble and to revive the heart of the contrite' *(Isaiah 57:15)*.

What is our response to God's goodness and love in coming so close to us through his Son, Jesus? St John tells us what happened at Jesus' first coming into the world. 'He came to his own and his own people did not accept him' *(John 1:11)*. What is your response to the coming of Jesus now? Is it one of indifference or rejection? The Pope pointed out what our response should be in the address quoted earlier: 'With gratitude for this condescension of God who desired to draw near to us... by addressing us in the very person of his only begotten Son, we repeat with humble and joyous faith: "You alone are the Holy One, you alone are the Lord, you alone are the Most High, Jesus Christ, with the Holy Spirit in the glory of God the Father, Amen"'. Pray that you will experience the reality of God's love in revealing Jesus to you this Christmas. Ask the Holy Spirit to help you. Repeat this prayer every day until Christmas: 'Holy Spirit come. Enlighten my mind that I might grasp the depths of God's love revealed in the birth of Jesus Christ. Help me to understand how he is God's provision for my salvation and how I desperately need him every day.'

At the end of Week 4
* Review the outline of Presentation 4.

* Review your notes on what God has been teaching you during your daily prayer and Scripture reading.

* Thank God for what he is teaching you.

* Make a resolution to be faithful to daily prayer and Scripture reading.

* Set aside time to prepare for confession. Try to have at least fifteen minutes when you will not be disturbed. Begin by asking the Holy Spirit to enlighten your mind so that you will know what sins you need to confess. Examine your conscience in a calm and peaceful way. Pray especially that you will be aware of 'hidden' sins that you have not noticed until now. Approach your confession with an attitude of confidence in God's mercy and forgiveness. After confession spend time thanking God for the love he has shown you in forgiving you your sins.

FAMILY ACTIVITIES FOR ADVENT

The purpose of this Advent programme is to enable participants to grow in holiness in preparation for the celebration of Christmas. This preparation cannot be confined to what happens in a meeting once a week or even to the participants' own prayer. It needs to extend also into family life, work situation and social life. We include here some suggestions for family activities during Advent. These activities, adapted if necessary, can also be used in convents or religious houses. Each family is free to select one or more of these activities or to devise new ones if they so wish.

1. 'The Word Among Us'

This booklet, published monthly, is a daily guide to the Christian life. A special edition is published each year for Advent and Lent. It contains a short essay for each week of Advent as well as a daily meditation on one of the readings of the Mass for that day. The essays will help you to gain a deeper understanding of the Incarnation and of how the coming of Jesus can affect your life. The meditations will help to guide your prayer and inspire you during the day.

The booklet can be used in a group setting. Many families use it at their evening meal. Before the meal one member of the family could read the Scripture for the day; another could read the meditation. Then, during the meal, family members could share and discuss what they understood from the readings. It is especially helpful, particularly when working with children and teenagers, if the parents prepare questions or comments ahead of time to help lead the conversation. For successful use of this approach, creativity is the key. In order to add variety to the activity, a member of the family could tell the Bible story in their own words or the reading could be shortened. Occasionally the children could be asked to prepare a drawing, illustrating the theme of the reading of the day. Remember, the purpose is to develop a greater interest in and deeper knowledge of Scripture. It will help if there is some fun attached to it.

The Word Among Us can be ordered from:-
  The Word Among Us,
  Turvey Abbey,
  Turvey,
  Bedfordshire MK43 8DE,
  England.

Special discounts are available for bulk orders.

2. The Advent Wreath

Wreaths have traditionally been used on joyous occasions as symbols of victory. The tradition of the Advent Wreath, normally consisting of a circle of evergreens, grew up in the western Church. The circular shape symbolises the eternal nature of God; the evergreens represent the continuing and everlasting life that comes from God through Christ. The four candles (three purple and one pink) mark the four weeks of Advent and attest to the truth of Jesus as the light of the world. The purple candles symbolise that Advent is a time of repentance, a time when we turn away from sin and towards God. The pink candle (for the third week of Advent) reminds us that we can rejoice because we are drawing near to Christmas Day. Placed in a prominent position within the home, the Advent Wreath can be a constant reminder of the real meaning of the season we are celebrating.

The lighting of the candles (one the first week, two the second and so on) could be done at the evening meal each day in conjunction with the reading of Scripture (e.g. the daily Scripture passage recommended in this Advent programme.) Another possibility is to use the Scripture passage for the day from *The Word Among Us* and to read the meditation based on it. The service could close with a formal or spontaneous prayer led by one member of the family. If it is not practical to do this at the evening meal, try to set aside time before or after the meal.

3. The crib

Many Churches set up a crib for the feast of Christmas. Increasingly, families are following this custom and setting up a small crib in their homes. The origin of the custom can be traced back to St Francis of Assisi (1181 - 1226) who, out of his great love for Jesus, the incarnate Son, re-enacted the birth of Jesus in a cave, at Greccio. Crib scenes can be used in a number of ways to help prepare for Christmas, especially if there are young children in the family. One way is to set up the crib at the beginning of Advent instead of waiting for the feast of Christmas. If this is done, the figure of the infant Jesus could be kept over until Christmas Eve. The children and the adults could write their good deeds on small slips of paper and place them in the crib to serve as straw for the infant Jesus (good deeds could include reading the Bible, being obedient, being kind to a friend, sharing a toy with a playmate). A variation of this is to draw an outline of a manger scene on a large piece of paper, instead of using a crib with figures. If they wish, the children could do the drawing. On each day of Advent, one portion of the scene could be coloured in to represent some good deed done during the day. Alternatively each child could have his or her own drawing if desired. Besides colouring in a portion of the scene, the children can also write (or have written for them) along the border of the picture the particular good deed they have done.

4. Making a Jesse tree

The Jesse tree is intended to be a visual depiction of the family tree of Jesus. It takes its inspiration from the words of the prophet Isaiah: 'There shall come forth a shoot from the stump of Jesse, and a branch shall grow out of his roots' *(Isaiah 11:1)*. In the middle ages some of the great cathedrals of Europe had stained glass windows which illustrated the ancestry of Jesus in the form of a tree growing out of Jesse (the father of King David). The descendants of Jesse were portrayed on scrolls like foliage branching out of one another. Such windows can still be seen in cathedrals today, such as those at Wells and York (England) and Chartres (France).

A Jesse tree can be made in any number of ways: a series of symbols or pictures pasted on to a large drawing of a tree; a miniature tree or shrub laden with symbols or signs representing Jesus' ancestry; perhaps a mobile hung from the ceiling with cut-outs representing items associated with the Lord's earthly ancestors. The varieties are almost endless. It could be decorated with drawings or names of Jesus' forebears. (See Matthew 1:1-17 or Luke 3:23-38.)

Each day a different member of the family might discuss the significance of one of the people depicted. This would give older children as well as adults an incentive to study the Scriptures to learn more about Jesus' ancestors. Some of the easier characters to start with are Noah, Ruth, Rahab, Jesse, David, Solomon, Hezechiah and Joseph. Each member of the family could be responsible for making a decoration and explaining its significance. For example, on 8 December (the Solemnity of the Immaculate Conception) one could draw a picture or symbol of Mary.

Creativity is important in making a Jesse tree interesting and fun for the whole family. All you need for this project are a few simple construction materials such as coat hangers, styrofoam, glue, rubber bands, ribbons, empty cardboard cartons, crayons, etc. and a little imagination.

5. Secret friends

This activity involves doing an act of kindness for another person and at the same time keeping it secret from that person. At the beginning of Advent, each family member writes his or her name on a piece of paper and the names of all are put in a bowl. Then each one draws out a name, and this person becomes their secret friend until Christmas. (Of course, if you draw out your own name you put it back and try for another.) It is important to keep the name a secret.

The next step is to search for ways of doing acts of kindness for your secret friend. The most valuable act of kindness is to pray every day for this person. Other acts of kindness would be to offer to do his/her household chores; buy a small gift that you know will be appreciated; allow your friend to choose which TV programme to watch. You can think of many other ideas that will help to bring happiness to your secret friend.

As Christmas Day approaches make a special card for your secret friend. Write on the card any Scripture passages which God has shown you in your prayer to be of particular importance for your friend. It is a good idea also to include a Scripture verse in the wishes you express on the card. On Christmas Eve or Christmas Day the card can be handed over to your secret friend, accompanied by an inexpensive gift. It should be arranged that all the family members hand over their cards (and gifts) at the same time (perhaps at the end of a family meal). It can be fun discovering who your secret friend is and trying to recall the acts of kindness done for you during Advent.

6. Decoration and blessing of the Christmas tree

The Christmas tree is often seen as a merely secular symbol in the home at Christmas. However, it can be a powerful sign of Christ's presence in the home and of the new life God gives us through his Son, Jesus Christ. One way to highlight its spiritual significance is to have a ceremony of blessing the Christmas tree. The blessing could take place when all the family are assembled and could be led by the father or mother. Other members of the family could be actively involved in the ceremony through hymn singing, Scripture readings and prayers of intercession. If desired, an additional ceremony could be added in celebration of lighting the Christmas tree. You might like to use all or some of the following format or, alternatively, to devise your own. A prayer has been included to accompany the lighting of the tree.

Suggested form of blessing:

a) *Opening hymn*

b) *Scripture reading*
(Suggestions: Luke 2:1-14; Luke 2:15-20; Luke 2:22-32; John 1:1-5; John 1:9-14.)

c) Prayer and blessing
Lord God, you sent your Son into the world
To free us from sin and bring us into your Kingdom.
Bless this green tree
And let it be a sign of the everlasting life that he has won for us.
Teach us so to live during this Christmas season
As to prepare for the everlasting life of heaven.
We make our prayer through Christ, Our Lord. Amen.

d) Prayers of intercession
(Short prayers of intercession could be composed and said by members of the family.)

e) Hymn
(Switch on Christmas lights.)

f) Prayer
Lord Jesus, you came into the world as a child on the first Christmas night.
You came to bring light to a world in darkness.
Enlighten our minds and hearts this Christmas season
So that we may know you and your love and mercy. Amen.

g) Closing hymn

7. Christmas cards
Christmas cards can bring joy to those who receive them and also help to highlight
the significance of the birth of Jesus. On the other hand they can be little more than
another aspect of the secular celebration of Christmas.

a) Sending Christmas cards
Those who have come to understand the meaning of Christmas in a deeper way can
use this custom to highlight the birth of the Saviour of the world. One way to do
this is to choose cards on which the illustrations and greetings are related to the real
meaning of Christmas. Many of the cards on sale today have more to do with the
secular than the religious celebration of Christmas, so you may need to search a little
to find suitable ones. Most religious bookshops carry a stock of the type of cards you
are looking for.
  Another way you can highlight the meaning of Christmas is by the kind of personal
greetings you write on your Christmas cards. You might like to express the wish that
your friends will enjoy 'the peace of Christ' or 'the new life of the Saviour'. You
will be able to think of several other appropriate greetings. Phrases like 'a merry
Christmas' can sound a bit hollow as a Christmas greeting. There are many short
greetings and prayers in Scripture that would be very suitable for your Christmas
cards and presents. Here are a few examples. You will probably be able to find many
more yourself.

> 'Ask, and it will be given to you; search, and you will find; knock and it
> will be opened to you. Everyone who asks receives; everyone who searches
> finds; everyone who knocks will have the door opened.' *(Matthew 7:7-8)*

'Come to me, all you who labour and are overburdened, and I will give you rest.' *(Matthew 11:28)*

'Blessed is he who is coming as King in the name of the Lord! Peace in heaven and glory in the highest heavens!' *(Luke 19:38)*

'Anyone who loves me will keep my word, and my Father will love him, and we shall come to him and make a home in him.' *(John 14:23)*

'Peace I bequeath to you; my own peace I give you, a peace which the world cannot give, this is my gift to you.' *(John 14:27)*

'For I am certain of this: neither death nor life, nor angels, nor principalities, nothing already in existence and nothing still to come... will be able to come between us and the love of God, known to us in Christ Jesus Our Lord.' *(Romans 8:38-39)*

'The grace of the Lord Jesus Christ, the love of God and the fellowship of the Holy Spirit be with you all.' *(2 Corinthians 13:14)*

'Glory be to him whose power, working in us, can do infinitely more than we can ask or imagine; glory be to him from generation to generation in the Church and in Christ Jesus for ever and ever. Amen.' *(Ephesians 3:20-21)*

'May grace be with all who love our Lord Jesus Christ, in life imperishable.' *(Ephesians 6:24)*

'Grace and peace to you from God our Father and the Lord Jesus Christ.' *(Philippians 1:2)*

'Never worry about anything; but tell God all your desires of every kind in prayer and petition shot through with gratitude, and the peace of God which is beyond our understanding will guard your hearts and your thoughts in Christ Jesus.' *(Philippians 4:6-7)*

'May the Lord turn your hearts towards the love of God and the perseverance of Christ.' *(2 Thessalonians 3:5)*

'May the Lord of peace himself give you peace at all times and in every way.' *(2 Thessalonians 3:16)*

b) Receiving Christmas cards
Sometimes Christmas cards are put away in a drawer as soon as the greeting is read. Frequently they are put on display or used as decorations in the home. Yet there are other ways in which they can be used. The family could choose an evening or a number of evenings during which a short time could be set aside for focusing on Christmas cards. As with many of the other activities the best time might be after the evening meal, when the whole family is gathered together. This activity could be approached in a variety of ways. If the illustrations or greetings on the cards relate

to the real meaning of Christmas, then their significance could be discussed. Some time could be spent in sharing thoughts about the people who sent the cards. If different members of the family have received cards from different friends, each could share something about the senders with the rest of the group. Afterwards the family could join together in praying for the needs of those who sent cards.

8. The Christmas candle
The old Irish custom of placing a lighted candle in the window on Christmas Eve is still practised in many areas. The lighted candle is intended to be a sign of welcome to the Saviour of the World. The lighting of the candle would be an excellent time for the whole family to gather together for prayer. This could include the singing of Christmas carols and a reading from Scripture. (Any of the passages suggested on page 46 would be suitable.) They could end by saying together The Apostles' Creed or The Angelus - a profession of faith in Jesus, the Saviour of the World.

SCRIPTURE PASSAGES FOR
'A STRUCTURE FOR PRAYER'

Matthew 5:23; 6:14-15
So then, if you are bringing your offering to the altar and there remember that your brother has something against you.... Yes, if you forgive others their failings, your heavenly Father will forgive you yours; but if you do not forgive others, your Father will not forgive your failings either.

Genesis 1:27-31
God created man in the image of himself, in the image of God he created him, male and female he created them. God blessed them, saying to them, 'Be fruitful, multiply, fill the earth and subdue it. Be masters of the fish of the sea, the birds of heaven and all the living creatures that move on earth.' God also said, 'Look, to you I give all the seed-bearing plants everywhere on the surface of the earth, and all the trees with seed-bearing fruit; this will be your food. And to all the wild animals, all the birds of heaven and all the living creatures that creep along the ground, I give all the foliage of the plants as their food.' And so it was. God saw all he had made, and indeed it was very good. Evening came and morning came: the sixth day.

1 John 4:10-11
Love consists in this: it is not we who loved God but God loved us and sent his Son to expiate our sins. My dear friends, if God loved us so much, we too should love each other.

John 3:16
For this is how God loved the world: he gave his only Son, so that everyone who believes in him may not perish but may have eternal life.

Ephesians 2:4-5
But God, being rich in faithful love, through the great love with which he loved us, even when we were dead in our sins, brought us to life with Christ - it is through grace that you have been saved.

Romans 5:12-18
Well then; it was through one man that sin came into the world, and through sin death, and thus death has spread through the whole human race because everyone has sinned. Sin already existed in the world before there was any law, even though sin is not reckoned when there is no law. Nonetheless death reigned over all from Adam to Moses, even over those whose sin was not the breaking of a commandment, as Adam's was. He prefigured the One who was to come... There is no comparison between the free gift and the offence. If death came to many through the offence of one man, how much greater an effect the grace of God has had, coming to so many and so plentifully as a free gift through the one man Jesus Christ! Again, there is no comparison between the gift and the offence of one man. One single offence brought condemnation, but now, after many offences, have come the free gift and so acquittal! It was by one man's offence that death came to reign over all, but how much greater

the reign in life of those who receive the fullness of grace and the gift of saving justice, through the one man, Jesus Christ. One man's offence brought condemnation on all humanity; and one man's good act has brought justification and life to all humanity.

1 Corinthians 15:20-26
In fact, however, Christ has been raised from the dead, as the first-fruits of all who have fallen asleep. As it was by one man that death came, so through one man has come the resurrection of the dead. Just as all die in Adam, so in Christ all will be brought to life, but all of them in their proper order: Christ the first-fruits, and next, at his coming, those who belong to him. After that will come the end, when he will hand over the kingdom to God the Father, having abolished every principality, every ruling force and power. For he is to be king until he has made his enemies his footstool, and the last of the enemies to be done away with is death, for he has put all things under his feet.

John 14:16,26; 16:7
I shall ask the Father and he will give you another Paraclete to be with you for ever.... But the Paraclete, the Holy Spirit, whom the Father will send in my name, will teach you everything and remind you of all I have said to you... Still, I am telling you the truth: it is for your own good that I am going, because unless I go, the Paraclete will not come to you; but if I go, I will send him to you.

Acts 2:1-11
When Pentecost day came round, they had all met together, when suddenly there came from heaven a sound as of a violent wind which filled the entire house in which they were sitting; and there appeared to them tongues as of fire; these separated and came to rest on the head of each of them. They were all filled with the Holy Spirit and began to speak different languages as the Spirit gave them power to express themselves.

   Now there were devout men living in Jerusalem from every nation under heaven, and at this sound they all assembled, and each one was bewildered to hear these men speaking his own language. They were amazed and astonished. 'Surely,' they said, 'all these men speaking are Galileans? How does it happen that each of us hears them in his own native language? Parthians, Medes and Elamites; people from Mesopotamia, Judaea and Cappadocia, Pontus and Asia, Phrygia and Pamphylia, Egypt and the parts of Libya round Cyrene; residents of Rome - Jews and proselytes alike - Cretans and Arabs; we hear them preaching in our own language about the marvels of God.'

Romans 8:34
Are we not sure that it is Christ Jesus, who died - yes and more, who was raised from the dead and is at God's right hand - and who is adding his plea for us?

Hebrews 7:25
It follows, then, that his power to save those who come to God through him is absolute, since he lives for ever to intercede for them.

1 John 2:1
My children, I am writing this to prevent you from sinning; but if anyone does sin, we have an advocate with the Father, Jesus Christ, the upright.

Matthew 16:27; 25:34
'For the Son of man is going to come in the glory of his Father with his angels, and then he will reward each one according to his behaviour.' 'Come, you whom my Father has blessed, take as your heritage the kingdom prepared for you since the foundation of the world.'

Matthew 7:7
Ask, and it will be given to you; search, and you will find; knock, and the door will be opened to you.

Colossians 3:16
Let the Word of Christ, in all its richness, find a home with you. Teach each other, and advise each other, in all wisdom. With gratitude in your hearts sing psalms and hymns and inspired songs to God.

Psalms 22; 95; 136
(You will find these psalms in your Bible.)

PRAYERS FOR DAILY USE

OUR FATHER

Our Father, who art in heaven,
Hallowed be thy name.
Thy Kingdom come.
Thy will be done on earth, as it is in
    heaven.
Give us this day our daily bread,
And forgive us our trespasses,
As we forgive those who trespass
    against us,
And lead us not into temptation,
But deliver us from evil. Amen.

HAIL MARY

Hail Mary, full of grace,
The Lord is with you.
Blessed are you among women,
And blessed is the fruit of your
    womb, Jesus.
Holy Mary, Mother of God,
Pray for us sinners,
Now and at the hour of our death.
    Amen.

GLORY BE TO THE FATHER

Glory be to the Father,
And to the Son,
And to the Holy Spirit;
As it was in the beginning,
Is now and ever shall be,
World without end. Amen.

THE APOSTLES' CREED

I believe in God, the Father
    almighty,
Creator of heaven and earth.

I believe in Jesus Christ, his only
    Son, our Lord.
He was conceived by the power of
    the Holy Spirit
And born of the Virgin Mary.
He suffered under Pontius Pilate,
Was crucified, died, and was buried.

He descended to the dead.
On the third day he rose again.
He ascended into heaven,
And is seated at the right hand of the
    Father.
He will come again to judge the
    living and the dead.

I believe in the Holy Spirit,
The holy catholic Church,
The communion of saints,
The forgiveness of sins,
The resurrection of the body,
And life everlasting. Amen.

THE CONFITEOR

I confess to almighty God,
And to you, my brothers and sisters,
That I have sinned through my own
    fault
In my thoughts and in my words,
In what I have done,
And in what I have failed to do;
And I ask blessed Mary, ever virgin,
All the angels and saints,
And you, my brothers and sisters,
To pray for me to the Lord our God.

ACT OF SORROW

O my God, I thank you for loving
    me.
I am sorry for all my sins:
For not loving others and not loving
    you.
Help me to live like Jesus and not
    sin again. Amen.

ACT OF SORROW (Alternative)

O my God, because you are so good,
I am very sorry that I have sinned
    against you,
And by the help of your grace I will
    not sin again. Amen.

THE MEMORARE

Remember,
O most gracious Virgin Mary,
That never was it known,
That anyone,
Who fled to your protection,
Implored your help,
Or sought your intercession,
Was left unaided.
Inspired with this confidence,
I fly to you,
O Virgin of Virgins, my Mother.
To you I come,
Before you I stand,
Sinful and sorrowful.
O Mother of the word incarnate,
Do not reject my petitions,
But graciously hear and answer
  them. Amen.

THE ANGELUS

(May be said morning, noon and
night, to put us in mind that God
the Son became man for our
salvation.)

V. The angel of the Lord declared to
    Mary:
R. And she conceived of the Holy
    Spirit.
    Hail Mary...
V. Behold the handmaid of the
    Lord:
R. Be it done unto me according to
    your word.
    Hail Mary...
V. And the Word was made flesh:
R. And dwelt among us.
    Hail Mary...
V. Pray for us, O holy Mother of
    God:
R. That we may be made worthy of
    the promises of Christ.

Let us pray:
Pour forth, we beseech you, O Lord,
Your grace into our hearts,
That we, to whom the Incarnation of
  Christ, your Son,

Was made known by the message of
  an angel,
May be brought by his passion and
  cross to the glory of his
  resurrection,
Through the same Christ our Lord.
  Amen.

May the divine assistance remain
  always with us,
And may the souls of the faithful
  departed,
Through the mercy of God,
Rest in peace. Amen.

HAIL, HOLY QUEEN

Hail, holy Queen, mother of mercy;
Hail, our life, our sweetness, and our
  hope!
To you do we cry, poor banished
  children of Eve;
To you do we send up our sighs,
  mourning and weeping
In this vale of tears.
Turn then, most gracious advocate,
Your eyes of mercy towards us;
And after this our exile,
Show to us the blessed fruit of your
  womb, Jesus.
O clement, O loving, O sweet Virgin
  Mary.
V. Pray for us, O holy Mother of
   God.
R. That we may be made worthy of
   the promises of Christ.

GRACE BEFORE AND AFTER
   MEALS

Bless us, O God, as we sit together.
Bless the food we eat today.
Bless the hands that made the food.
Bless us, O God. Amen.

Thank you, God, for the food we
  have eaten.
Thank you, God, for all our friends.
Thank you, God, for everything.
Thank you, O God. Amen.

GRACE BEFORE AND AFTER MEALS (Alternative)

Bless us, O Lord,
And these your gifts,
Which we are about to receive
From your bounty.
Through Christ our Lord. Amen.

We give you thanks, almighty God,
For all your benefits,
Who live and reign,
For ever and ever.
May the souls of the faithful
    departed,
Through the mercy of God,
Rest in peace. Amen.

MORNING OFFERING

O my God,
I offer you all my thoughts,
Words, actions and sufferings;
And I beseech you to give me your
    grace,
That I may not offend you this day,
But may faithfully serve you,
And do your holy will in all things.
    Amen.

MORNING OFFERING (Alternative)

Father in heaven, you love me,
You are with me night and day.
I want to love you always
In all I do and say.
I'll try to please you, Father.
Bless me through the day. Amen.

PRAYER TO THE HOLY SPIRIT

Come, Holy Spirit, fill the hearts of
    the faithful
And kindle in them the fire of your
    love.
Send forth your Spirit, and they shall
    be created,
And you will renew the face of the
    earth.

O God, who has taught the hearts of
    the faithful
By the light of the Holy Spirit,
Grant us in the same spirit to be
    truly wise
And ever to rejoice in his
    consolation,
Through Christ Our Lord. Amen.